Dig It:
Ancient Egypt

Courtney Acampora

Silver Dolphin

Silver Dolphin Books

An imprint of Printers Row Publishing Group
10350 Barnes Canyon Road, Suite 100, San Diego, CA 92121
www.silverdolphinbooks.com

Printers Row Publishing Group is a division of Readerlink Distribution Services, LLC.
Silver Dolphin Books is a registered trademark of Readerlink Distribution Services, LLC.

All notations of errors or omissions should be addressed to Silver Dolphin Books, Editorial Department, at
the above address.

ISBN: 978-1-68412-318-6

Manufactured, printed, and assembled in Heshan, China. First printing, December 2017. HH/12/17.
21 20 19 18 17   1 2 3 4 5

Toy manufactured in Hong Kong.

Written by Courtney Acampora
Designed by Dynamo Limited

Image Credits:
Thinkstock, SuperStock, Inc, Getty Images

Contents

Ancient Egypt

When one thinks about ancient Egypt, thoughts of magnificent **pharaohs** and mysterious mummies come to mind. While these are both true, ancient Egypt was even more than that—it was an advanced **civilization**. In fact, their use and development of science and mathematics has served as the basis for those we use today. Around 6000 to 5000 BCE, people from less fertile areas in Africa and southwest Asia settled along the Nile River. The ancient Egyptian civilization lasted over 3,000 years, and was one of the longest-lasting civilizations in the world.

Today, thousands of years after pharaohs ruled the vast deserts, stunning engravings, paintings, and sculptures still exist. The discovery of treasures in ancient Egypt in the late eighteenth century inspired a branch of study called **Egyptology**. Egyptologists learn about ancient Egyptian life by studying surviving art, architecture, objects, and writings.

So much can be learned from these **artifacts**, whether it's about royalty, beliefs about gods, jewelry and clothing, or family life. Get ready for an Egyptian adventure — one filled with giant **pyramids**, magnificent temples, and the sandy shores of the Nile River. There are many more Egyptian treasures just waiting to be uncovered — can you dig it?

River of Life

When ancient Egypt began to be inhabited, people settled along the Nile River. The Nile River, flowing 4,132 miles, is the longest river in the world. It begins near the **equator** in Africa where it flows north into the Mediterranean Sea. Located in northern Africa, the Nile River is surrounded by a hot, dry desert. Inhabitants settled near the edges of the Nile so Egypt ended up being quite narrow. The Nile River was crucial to ancient Egyptian life, providing the inhabitants with fish, fresh water, and the ability to cultivate crops.

Each year, the Nile River flooded the surrounding valleys, making the soil rich for farming. White birds called ibises flew up from the south, and when they arrived the Egyptians knew that the floods would soon follow. The ancient Egyptians had three seasons based on the flooding of the Nile River.

Ibis

1 Inundation (July-October): Flooding of the river. The New Year occurred in mid-July when the Nile began to rise and eventually flood.

2 Planting (October-mid-February): After the flood, the land began to emerge again. It was then filled with nutrients from the river's silt. Seeds were then planted.

3 Harvest (February-June): The busy period when ancient Egyptians gathered all of the crops.

In addition to providing the ancient Egyptians with water and food, the Nile River also allowed for the transportation of people and goods up and down the river. Skiffs were boats made from tied **papyrus** reeds. The skiffs were used for hunting, fishing, and traveling short distances. By 3000 BCE, the ancient Egyptians began building boats out of wood.

After the water drained away, farmers planted seeds. By 3000 BCE, farmers began digging **irrigation** canals that carried water farther out to dry areas. This increased the Egyptians' amount of fertile farming land. The ancient Egyptians grew wheat to make flour, fruits such as dates and figs, flax that was woven into fabric called linen or made into ropes, and vegetables such as lettuce, radishes, asparagus, and cucumbers. Many of their crops could be stored for later use. The papyrus reeds that lined the banks of the Nile were used for constructing mats, boats, and paper.

Daily Life

As the Egyptian civilization grew more complex, people took on other jobs besides farmer or scribe. The social structure of ancient Egypt can be viewed like a pyramid. At the top of the social structure were the pharaohs. Pharaohs were the rulers and controlled all of the land. Temples and pyramids were constructed to honor the pharaohs. Under the pharaohs were the priests and nobles. Beneath the priests and nobles were scribes and government officials, then artisans and merchants, then farmers, and lastly laborers and slaves.

SCRIBES

Scribes recorded information for government and religious leaders. They began their extensive schooling around five years old. They learned **hieroglyphs**, the ancient Egyptian writing. Scribes learned hieroglyphs by copying them over and over again. At first, scribes practiced their writing on wood, stone, and pottery. After much practice, the scribes then began writing on papyrus, a type of paper made from papyrus reeds. The early hieroglyphs consisted of 700 characters which eventually grew to around 6,000 characters.

Scribes recorded grain and food supplies, collected taxes, and recorded history and important events. Their supplies included pens made from sharpened reeds and red and black inks.

ARTISANS AND MERCHANTS

Artisans made pottery, jewelry, linen cloth, and metal goods. Because the ancient Egyptians didn't always have currency, they depended on trading in order to get goods. The Nile River was used to move people up and down river so they could exchange goods with others.

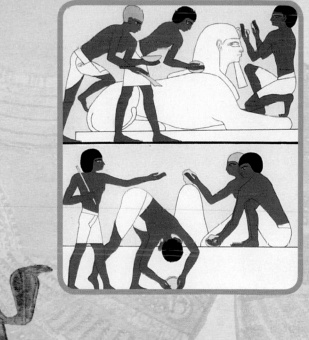

The most skilled artisans were stonecarvers. They created the many statues, engravings, and reliefs in tombs, temples, and on monuments. Stonecarvers often had to work with tough rock like granite. They first used a hard rock to break away rock and create the initial shape. Then details were added and stonecarvers refined the shape with stone tools and copper chisels. Finally, stonecarvers polished the object.

Daily Life

FARMERS

The lives of farmers revolved around the Nile River and its seasons of flood, planting, and harvest. During planting season, farmers went out in the fields in pairs. By 3000 BCE, Egyptian farmers began using cattle-drawn plows. While the cattle pulled the plow, the farmer dropped the seeds.

During the planting season, farmers sowed the fields with seeds such as wheat and barley—key crops used for making bread and beer. The farmers irrigated the land to make sure the crops received plenty of water.

DID YOU KNOW?

WHEN HERDING CATTLE ACROSS WATER, FARMERS CHANTED SPELLS TO WARD OFF CROCODILES.

LABORERS AND SLAVES

Laborers and slaves were at the bottom of the social pyramid, and they ended up in their position because they owed debt, committed a crime, or were captured in war.

Slaves worked as servants in the households of pharaohs, nobles, or priests. They had some rights such as owning land, hiring their own servant, or marrying someone who wasn't a slave. Slaves that weren't as lucky worked in the hot, North African deserts mining gold and copper.

At Home with the Egyptians

Family life was very important in ancient Egypt. Everyone in ancient Egypt married—even gods and goddesses. Families consisted of several children; boys trained in the same line of work as their fathers, and girls stayed at home and learned from their mothers. The main role of women was to care for the children at home, but they could also weave cloth and work with their husbands in fields or workshops. Upper-class women could be in charge of temples and could perform religious ceremonies. Women in ancient Egypt had many of the same rights as men, and they could own and manage their own property.

CHILDREN

Children were very important to ancient Egyptians. Adults used spells and charms to protect their children. Boys and girls from wealthier families went to schools run by scribes or priests. Like children today, kids in ancient Egypt played with toys such as wooden boats, played games such as leap frog, and enjoyed wrestling and dancing. Adults and children liked to play a popular board game called senet. In this game, the players threw sticks to see how many squares to move their game piece.

Houses

Wealthier ancient Egyptians had fancier homes with pools and gardens, and furniture such as bed frames and cushions. Farmers could rent the land that they worked on, and they lived in villages along the Nile. Their homes had one bedroom and had roofs made of palms. Workers lived in homes made of mud brick with a courtyard where they kept their animals. Their flat roof was used for socializing and sleeping.

Egyptian Style

The ancient Egyptians were very stylish. They wore linen clothes and wore sandals made out of leather or papyrus. Men who worked in the fields wore linen kilts while they worked. Both men and women wore jewelry made from precious stones such as amethyst, onyx, turquoise, copper, gold, and seashells. Hygiene was also important to the ancient Egyptians—they bathed and used oils, perfumes, razors, and mirrors. Children had shaved heads except for a lock of hair that would hang down the right side of their heads. Important people wore wigs, and both men and women wore makeup. Green and black powders, called kohl, lined their eyes. In addition to making them beautiful, research suggests that their eye makeup prevented eye infections that were common along the Nile River. Makeup was also believed to have magical powers and signified that they were protected by the gods Horus and Ra.

Pets

In addition to children, pets were also an important part of family life. Popular pets included cats, dogs, ducks, pigeons, and even monkeys! Cats were especially popular pets in Egypt. The ancient Egyptians believed cats were special like their gods. They believed cats protected their house and children. They dressed their cats in jewels, and even worshipped a cat goddess. The ancient Egyptians created many paintings and sculptures to honor cats. When their pets died, the ancient Egyptians mummified them. When a family's cat died, the owners shaved off their eyebrows. They continued to mourn the cat's death until their eyebrows grew back!

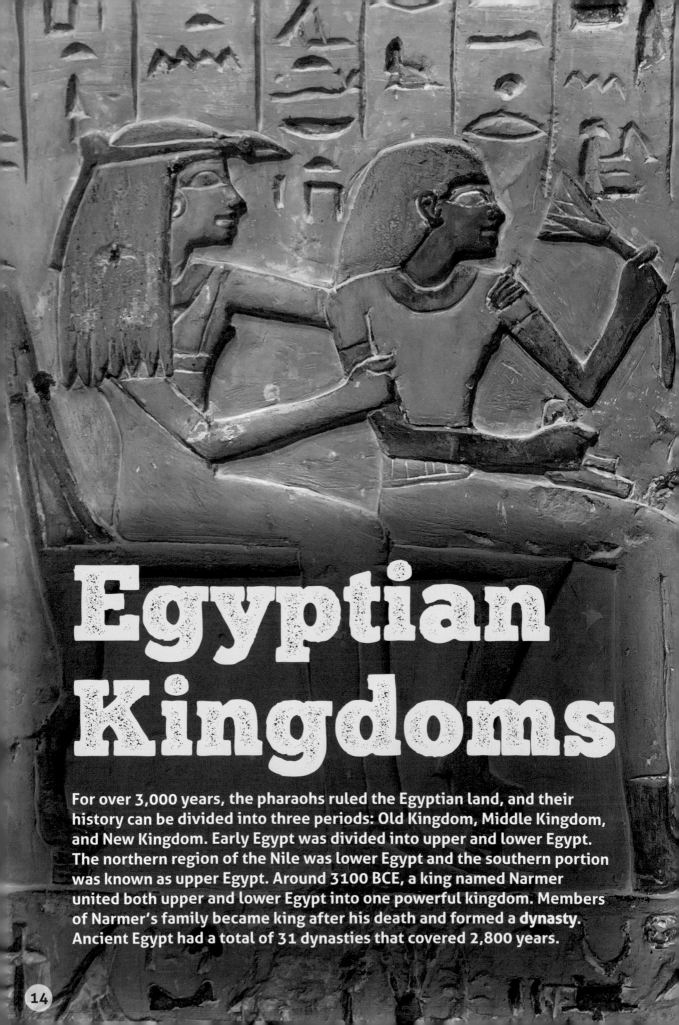

Egyptian Kingdoms

For over 3,000 years, the pharaohs ruled the Egyptian land, and their history can be divided into three periods: Old Kingdom, Middle Kingdom, and New Kingdom. Early Egypt was divided into upper and lower Egypt. The northern region of the Nile was lower Egypt and the southern portion was known as upper Egypt. Around 3100 BCE, a king named Narmer united both upper and lower Egypt into one powerful kingdom. Members of Narmer's family became king after his death and formed a **dynasty**. Ancient Egypt had a total of 31 dynasties that covered 2,800 years.

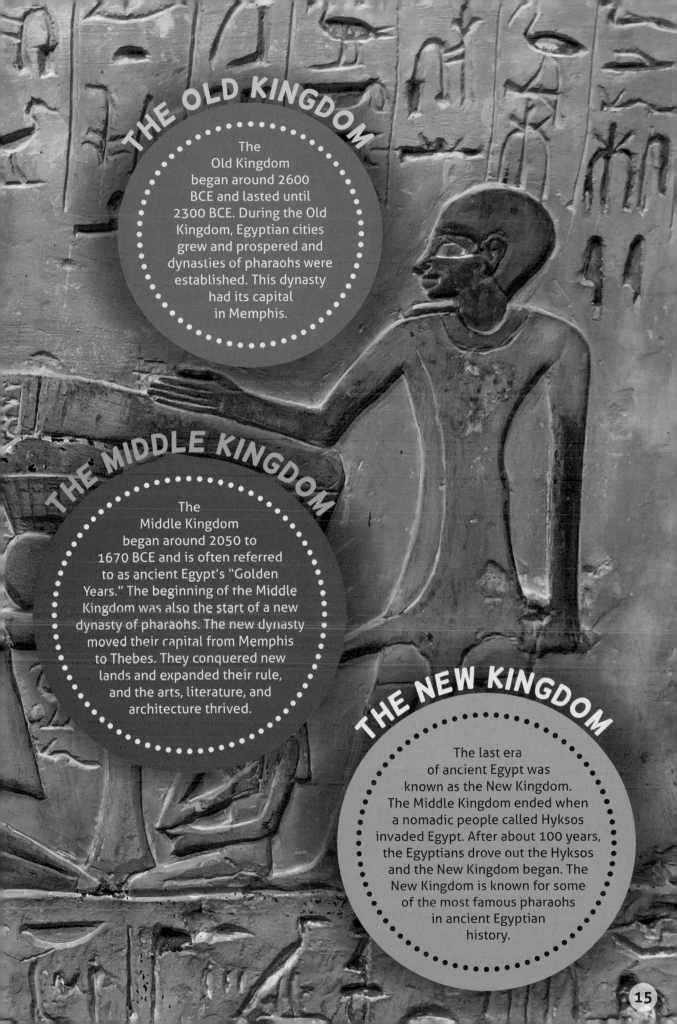

THE OLD KINGDOM

The Old Kingdom began around 2600 BCE and lasted until 2300 BCE. During the Old Kingdom, Egyptian cities grew and prospered and dynasties of pharaohs were established. This dynasty had its capital in Memphis.

THE MIDDLE KINGDOM

The Middle Kingdom began around 2050 to 1670 BCE and is often referred to as ancient Egypt's "Golden Years." The beginning of the Middle Kingdom was also the start of a new dynasty of pharaohs. The new dynasty moved their capital from Memphis to Thebes. They conquered new lands and expanded their rule, and the arts, literature, and architecture thrived.

THE NEW KINGDOM

The last era of ancient Egypt was known as the New Kingdom. The Middle Kingdom ended when a nomadic people called Hyksos invaded Egypt. After about 100 years, the Egyptians drove out the Hyksos and the New Kingdom began. The New Kingdom is known for some of the most famous pharaohs in ancient Egyptian history.

Gods and Goddesses

The ancient Egyptians believed in many gods and thought that every natural occurrence was caused by the gods—whether it was food supply, weather, or death. Certain areas throughout Egypt had their own local gods.

Ra

The name "Ra" is the Egyptian word meaning Sun. Ra was called the Sun god, the ultimate source of light, energy, and life. In Egyptian myth, the most important event was the first sunrise. This event brought about the creation of the cosmos, when darkness left the earth. Just as the Sun rises and sets each day, the god Ra was born every morning to his sky goddess mother and passed back to her each day. He was King of the Gods on earth and then in heaven.

Osiris

Osiris was the god of death and the king of the underworld. He was represented as a mummified king holding a hooked staff and flail. The color of his skin, black or green, symbolizes Osiris's connection to death and the regeneration of plant life. Legend says that Osiris was likely killed by his brother Seth out of his own jealousy for the throne. Isis, wife of Osiris, with the help of Ra, tried to bring him back to life. But instead, Osiris traveled to the underworld and became king of the dead.

Sobek

Sobek was honored as a god of water. He was called the Lord of the Nile. He often appeared as a crocodile or a man with the head of a crocodile wearing an atef crown. Nile crocodiles were one of the largest reptiles in the world during ancient Egyptian times. Those who worked near the Nile River feared these large beasts. If caught, the body would be devoured. In death, ancient Egyptians required a physical body for the next life. Fishermen, in particular, revered Sobek and made him their patron god who would protect them as they worked along the Nile.

Isis

To the ancient Egyptians, Isis was perceived as the great mother and a patron goddess of marriage, fertility, motherhood, magic, and medicine. Her priestesses were healers and midwives. She was the wife of Osiris and mother of Horus. She is depicted wearing different headdresses: wearing one representing a throne, or wearing a vulture headdress with a serpent, or wearing a double crown representing Upper and Lower Egypt. As a goddess of magic, many people looked to her for problem-solving spells.

Horus, the Younger

Son of Osiris and Isis, Horus was the god of the sky. He was represented as a falcon and was viewed as the divine protector of the king. He had many other duties as the avenger of wrongs and the defender of order. Horus is credited with uniting Upper and Lower Egypt. During a battle for the throne of Egypt, Horus lost one of his eyes. It was restored to him and a symbol called the Eye of Horus became a symbol of protection.

Anubis

The god often depicted as a man with the head of a jackal is Anubis. He was feared by the ancient Egyptians. Anubis was primarily associated with death. He guarded graves from the carrion eaters who would dig up the newly buried. He also presided over the dead on their way to the underworld. He was called the "Master of Secrets" because he knew the secrets of mummification — the embalming process and the bandaging of the body. In addition, Anubis performed the Opening of the Mouth ritual. This ceremony gave back the senses to the mummy it once had in life.

Thoth

Thoth was the god of wisdom. He was just and incorruptible. Thoth was also the god who invented writing and different languages for humans. He was depicted as a baboon, as an ibis, or as an ibis-headed man. Thoth was the reporter to the god Ra. He observed and wrote down everything that happened each day. Thus, he was the recordkeeper to the gods.

Temples for the Gods

Most towns had their own temples that were dedicated to the local god or goddess. Other chapels were constructed to worship other important gods. Temples followed similar building plans. They featured a courtyard and reception room for the public, with smaller rooms that were only open to a select few. The most important room in the temple, the Holy of Holies, was only open to the priest and pharaoh. A statue or image of the god was included in the temple, and it was believed that the god resided there. The priests performed rituals for the gods and offered food, drinks, and clothing.

LUXOR TEMPLE

The temple at Luxor was part of the ancient city of Thebes, a capital of ancient Egypt. It was built over hundreds of years by several pharaohs including Amenhotep III and Ramses II. It was dedicated to the god Amon, who was the king of the gods. The ancient Egyptians believed that the god Amon experienced rebirth during the pharaoh's annual reenacted coronation ceremony. The main entrance to the temple was flanked by two giant statues of Ramses II.

Temple of Edfu

Temple of Edfu

Dedicated to the god Horus, the temple of Edfu is the second-largest temple in Egypt. It was one of the latest built temples, constructed in 257-37 BCE. The colonnaded section of the temple was used as the site of the annual Festival of Coronation, which reenacted the birth of Horus. There was also a Court of Offerings where people could give gifts to the god.

Writing

Around 3000 BCE, the ancient Egyptians created a writing system using hieroglyphs. Hieroglyphs were picture symbols that represented sounds, words, and ideas. These symbols formed meaningful messages that decorated statues, tomb walls, and more. The ancient Egyptians believed that hieroglyphs and writing were a gift from Thoth, the god of wisdom.

DID YOU KNOW?

THE ROSETTA STONE HAS BEEN HOUSED IN THE BRITISH MUSEUM SINCE 1802. DURING WORLD WAR II IT WAS MOVED TO ANOTHER LOCATION FOR PROTECTION.

When the French emperor Napoleon and his army spent time in Egypt at the end of eighteenth century, they discovered a mysterious stone that has served as one of the most important artifacts in history. In 1799, they discovered a carved stone slab in Rosetta, a town near Alexandria. The Rosetta Stone had three distinct languages carved into it: Egyptian hieroglyphs, Egyptian demotic (the everyday language), and ancient Greek.

ROSETTA STONE

The Rosetta Stone was translated by British scholar Thomas Young and French scholar Jean-François Champollion. Using the Greek text, they were able to decode the hieroglyphs. The Rosetta Stone was originally written by a council of priests and the 14-year-old pharaoh Ptolemy V.

Hieroglyphs

A	F	KH	K	Y
A	M	KH CH	G	Y
I	N	SZ	T	UW
UW	R	S	TJ	M
B	H	SH	D	N
P	H	K	DJ	L

The Book of the Dead

In addition to the Rosetta Stone, another important written document in ancient Egypt was *The Book of the Dead*. This important collection of texts featured spells that helped the deceased safely get to the afterlife. Scribes copied the spells on papyrus and they were sold for burial use. The spells were placed inside the tomb, or sometimes rolled up with the mummified body.

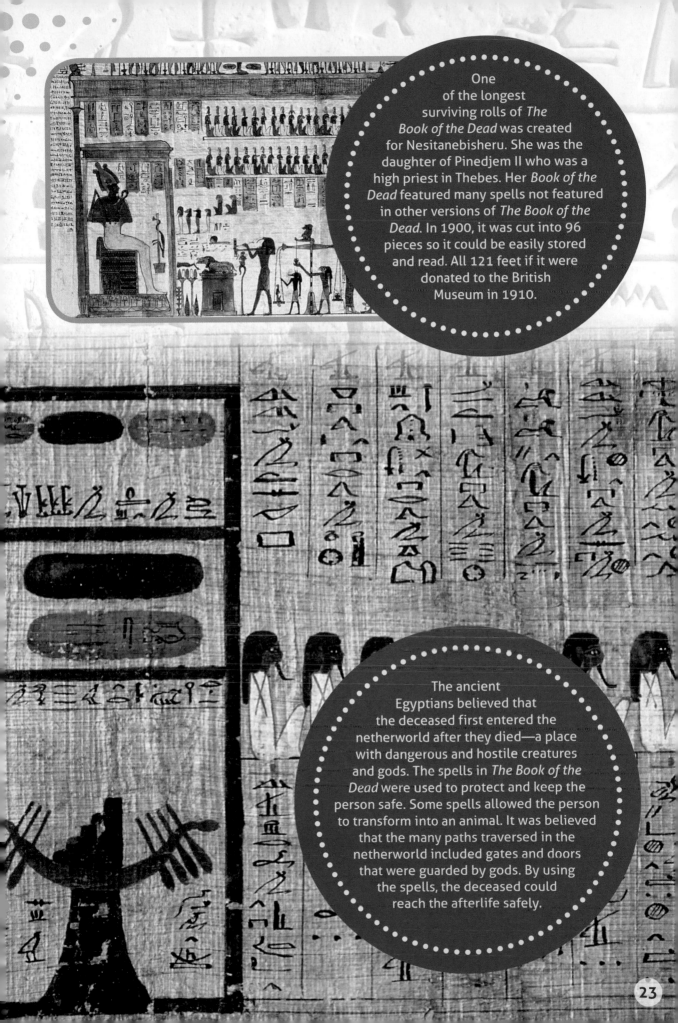

One of the longest surviving rolls of *The Book of the Dead* was created for Nesitanebisheru. She was the daughter of Pinedjem II who was a high priest in Thebes. Her *Book of the Dead* featured many spells not featured in other versions of *The Book of the Dead*. In 1900, it was cut into 96 pieces so it could be easily stored and read. All 121 feet if it were donated to the British Museum in 1910.

The ancient Egyptians believed that the deceased first entered the netherworld after they died—a place with dangerous and hostile creatures and gods. The spells in *The Book of the Dead* were used to protect and keep the person safe. Some spells allowed the person to transform into an animal. It was believed that the many paths traversed in the netherworld included gates and doors that were guarded by gods. By using the spells, the deceased could reach the afterlife safely.

Old Kingdom:
Pharaohs

Pharaohs were ancient Egyptian rulers. Even though the word "pharaoh" is well-known today, ancient Egyptian kings and queens were not called pharaohs during their time. Today, "pharaoh" is a generic word for Egyptian royalty, and it actually translates to "great house," which was used to describe the king's palace.

Pharaohs were worshipped alongside gods, as it was believed the pharaohs could communicate with the gods. Important statues of the pharaohs were made, and monuments were built in their honor. When they died, their bodies were placed in large and intricate tombs.

Pharaohs wore special clothes to show their power and wealth. Pharaohs wore a striped head cloth called a nemes. A jeweled, gold cobra was placed on their crown. Pharaohs also wore a fake beard. If the pharaoh was female, she wore a beard too!

Pharaohs were usually related. When a pharaoh died, his oldest son became the new pharaoh. When a pharaoh didn't have a son, a male relative could become the next pharaoh. The pharaoh owned a lot of Egypt's land and was responsible for the people's well-being. Women could become pharaohs too. If their husband died and their son was too young to rule, the woman could rule as a pharaoh.

Old Kingdom:
The Great Pyramids

The ancient Egyptian pyramids were the largest manmade structures ever built. They were built as burial places for pharaohs. It was believed that the pyramids, with their sloped sides, helped the dead pharaoh climb to the heavens.

In 2630 BCE, King Djoser built one of the first pyramids over his tomb. Unlike later pyramids, Djoser's was a step pyramid and consisted of giant steps that formed the sides. Eighty years later, construction began on the largest and most famous Egyptian pyramids ever built. The pharaoh Khufu built the first and largest pyramid of the complex. His son, Khafre, built the second pyramid that also included the Great Sphinx. The smallest pyramid of the complex was built by the pharaoh Menkaure.

Khufu's pyramid is almost 500 feet tall. It took more than twenty years to build, included over two million bricks, and was built by 20,000 workers. The workers were skilled and well-fed and most likely lived in nearby communities. Each pyramid included hidden chambers to keep the pharaoh's body safe. Eventually, pharaohs stopped building pyramids because grave robbers would break in and steal treasure in the tombs. By the New Kingdom, pharaohs built discreet tombs in an area called the Valley of the Kings.

DID YOU KNOW?
THE PYRAMIDS OF GIZA ARE ONE OF THE SEVEN WONDERS OF THE WORLD.

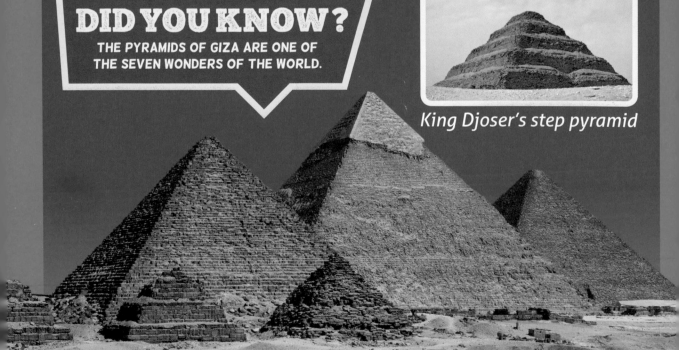

King Djoser's step pyramid

THE GREAT SPHINX

The Great Sphinx is a giant monument that is situated in front of Khafre's pyramid. A sphinx is a creature with a human head and a lion's body. It was built to guard the pharaoh's pyramid, and the sphinx's face was carved to resemble Khafre. The lion was a royal Egyptian symbol, so it would have also emphasized Khafre's power. At 241 feet long and 66 feet high, the Great Sphinx is the largest stone statue in Egypt.

DID YOU KNOW?

THE GREAT SPHINX WAS ORIGINALLY PAINTED BRIGHT COLORS INCLUDING BLUE AND RED!

The Great Sphinx was carved out of one giant piece of limestone. It would have taken hundreds of workers several years to finish the statue. When the Great Sphinx was carved, it had a head cloth with a sacred serpent that was a symbol of supreme power. But over time, parts of the Sphinx have broken off or been worn away.

Until 1817, the Great Sphinx was buried in sand up to its shoulders. An explorer from Genoa, Giovanni Battista, and his 160-person crew began digging out the Great Sphinx. However, the statue wasn't completely uncovered until the 1930s.

The Afterlife

The ancient Egyptians believed in the afterlife, the next stage after life on Earth. Before they could obtain their **immortality**, the deceased's body was overseen by a priest who performed the "Opening of the Mouth" ceremony. It was believed that the ceremony restored the deceased's senses, especially speech, which would be necessary in the underworld.

Osiris, the god of the underworld, met the deceased in the Hall of Judgment. In front of 42 other gods, the deceased spoke and plead for immortality. Their heart, which was kept intact during mummification, was weighed on a scale against a feather. The feather represented justice, and a perfectly balanced scale meant that the deceased had gained immortality.

The underworld was thought to be a scary place, so objects, like *The Book of the Dead*, were helpful in providing special spells to protect the deceased and help them safely navigate through the underworld. The next important stop on the road to the afterlife was the Hall of Judgment, where the weighing of the heart ceremony took place.

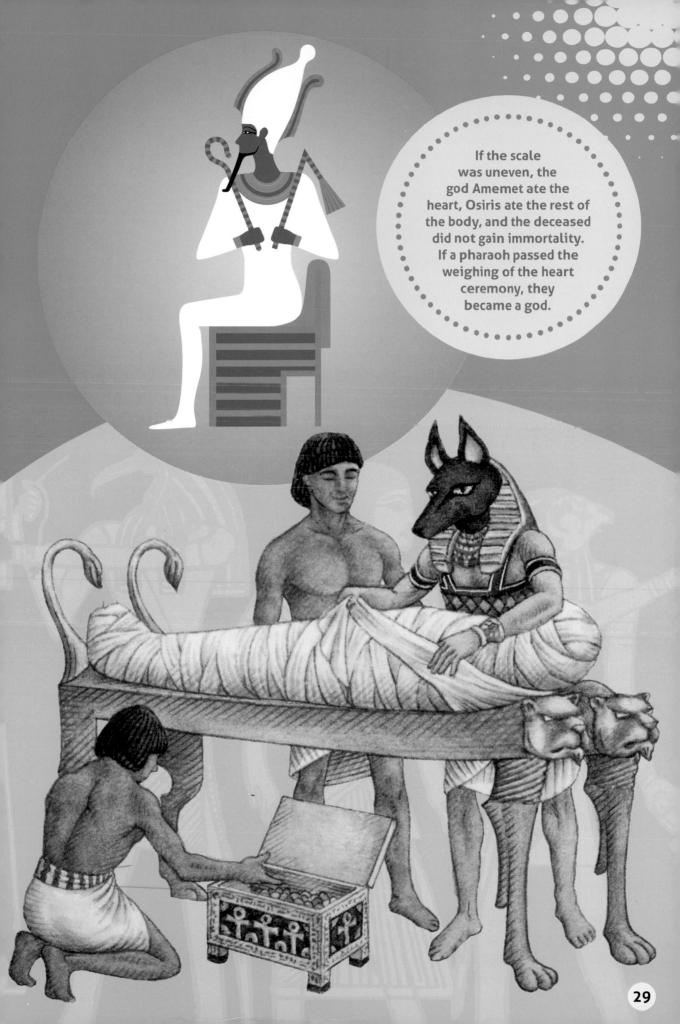

If the scale was uneven, the god Amemet ate the heart, Osiris ate the rest of the body, and the deceased did not gain immortality. If a pharaoh passed the weighing of the heart ceremony, they became a god.

Mummification

The ancient Egyptians practiced mummification, a way of preparing the body for the afterlife. The process of mummification dates back as early as 4100 BCE. Amazingly, many mummies are still so well-preserved today that it's possible to see what the person looked like long ago. Some bodies of ancient Egyptians still have skin, hair, bones, and soft tissues!

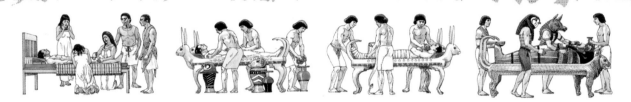

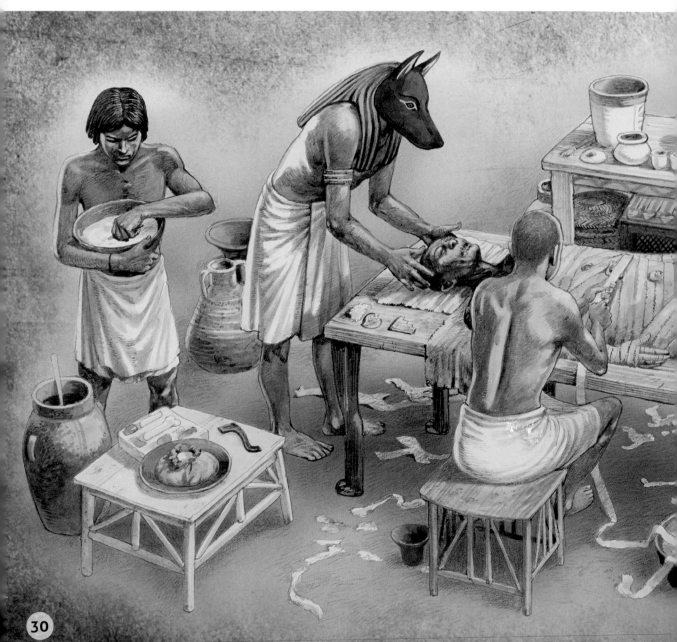

It's important to note that not all ancient Egyptians were mummified. Mummification was an expensive process reserved for pharaohs, nobility, and officials. The common people were buried in the desert. For those who could afford mummification, when a family member died, their body was transported to a wabet, which translates to "safe place." The wabet was typically a tent where the embalming process took place. The wabet was located away from the village, farther out in the desert.

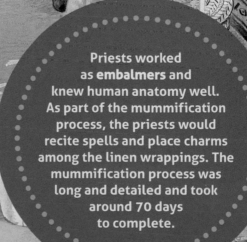

Priests worked as **embalmers** and knew human anatomy well. As part of the mummification process, the priests would recite spells and place charms among the linen wrappings. The mummification process was long and detailed and took around 70 days to complete.

The most important part of preserving the dead was to make the deceased look as lifelike as possible, since they would need their body in the afterlife. The first step was to make an incision on the left side of the abdomen to remove the lungs, liver, intestines, and stomach. The brain was removed through the nose with a hooked instrument. The brain was thrown away because the ancient Egyptians believed that the brain was useless. The heart, however, was left inside the body because they believed it was where a person's spirit and soul was kept.

CANOPIC JARS

The other organs were removed from the body and placed in special containers called canopic jars. The canopic jars were ornately decorated and often shaped like animals, such as jackals or hawks. These jars were placed beside the deceased and buried with the body since the organs would be needed in the afterlife.

DRYING

In order to preserve the body in its most lifelike form, all moisture needed to be removed from the body. To do this, natron, a natural salt substance was placed all over the body and it was left to dry out for 40 days. After the body was properly dried, the salt was washed away and the body was stuffed with linens and sawdust to give the body shape. Some organs were also placed back in the body to give it more shape.

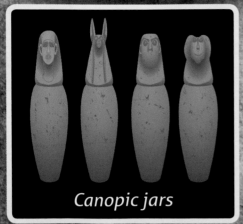

Canopic jars

DID YOU KNOW?

THE EGYPTIANS NOT ONLY MUMMIFIED HUMANS—ANIMALS WERE MUMMIFIED TOO! CATS WERE PRECIOUS PETS IN ANCIENT EGYPT, SO THEY WERE MUMMIFIED SO THEY COULD JOIN THEIR OWNERS IN THE AFTERLIFE.

The last step of mummification was to wrap the body in linens. Often, hundreds of yards of linens were needed to cover the body. While the embalmer wrapped the body, they also placed special amulets and charms in the wrapping to protect the body in the underworld. The finished mummy was placed in multiple coffins, then inside of a large, stone **sarcophagus**. Treasures, food, clothes, and drinks were placed with the mummy. The ancient Egyptians believed they needed these items in the afterlife. Later in Egyptian history, masks were placed over the mummy's face. The masks of pharaohs were made of gold and precious gems.

Prayer Ceremony

Once the body was ready to be placed in a tomb, a priest would perform prayers in front of the entrance of the tomb. This is also when the priest performed the Opening of the Mouth ceremony. During the Opening of the Mouth ceremony, the priest would use special ritual tools to touch the deceased's lips. This would allow them to speak, breathe, eat, and drink in the afterlife. The sarcophagus and all other objects and treasures were placed inside the tomb and it was sealed up.

New Kingdom: Hatshepsut

Queen Hatshepsut was the first female pharaoh. She became pharaoh when her husband died, and she ruled alongside her stepson Thutmose III. In 1472 BCE, she declared herself the sole pharaoh of Egypt. Hatshepsut used war to expand her territory and focused on trade expeditions. She began trading east near the Red Sea, where goods such as exotic spices, herbs, and wood were brought back. She also had **obelisks** built that were decorated with hieroglyphs to celebrate her accomplishments and power. After ruling for 15 years, Hatshepsut mysteriously disappeared. Her stepson, Thutmose III became pharaoh and tried to destroy monuments and records of Hatshepsut's rule.

Hatshepsut's Memorial Temple

Hatshepsut's Memorial Temple is one of the most spectacular buildings from the New Kingdom. The three-terraced temple was constructed at the base of a limestone cliff in western Thebes near the Valley of the Kings. The temple was dedicated to the god Amon, and statues and paintings of Hatshepsut decorated the interior and exterior of the temple. The reliefs inside the temple depicted Hatshepsut's coronation and divine birth.

New Kingdom:
King Tut

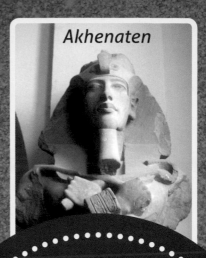

Akhenaten

King Tut is one of the most famous pharaohs from ancient Egypt. "Tut" is short for Tutankhamen. He is nicknamed the "boy king" because he became king at only eight years old. Tutankhamen did not live a long life; he died at just nineteen years old.

King Tut became pharaoh in 1332 BCE. He became king after his father, Akhenaten died. When Akhenaten was king, Egypt was a chaotic place. Akhenaten replaced the traditional worship of the god Amon with his own deity, Aten. Once Akhenaten died and Tut took over the throne, he restored the old religion and ways and brought order back to Egypt. Since many temples dedicated to Amon were destroyed when Akhenaten was pharaoh, King Tut restored the temples during his reign.

When King Tut died suddenly as a teenager, there wasn't a tomb constructed for him yet. Many scholars believe that King Tut was laid to rest in a tomb meant for someone else.

مقبرة توت عنخ آمون

TOMB OF TUT ANKH AMON
NO. 62

Diseased King

In recent years, scientists have uncovered more and more clues regarding King Tut's premature death. It is believed that King Tut had a bone disorder, called Köhler disease, that deformed his left foot. Among the treasure that was buried in his tomb, 130 walking sticks were also included in the tomb. This suggests that King Tut had difficulty walking and had to use a walking stick. In 2010, scientists studying King Tut discovered malaria, a deadly disease carried by mosquitos, in his remains. Finally, King Tut's parents were siblings, which would account for many of the illnesses he had.

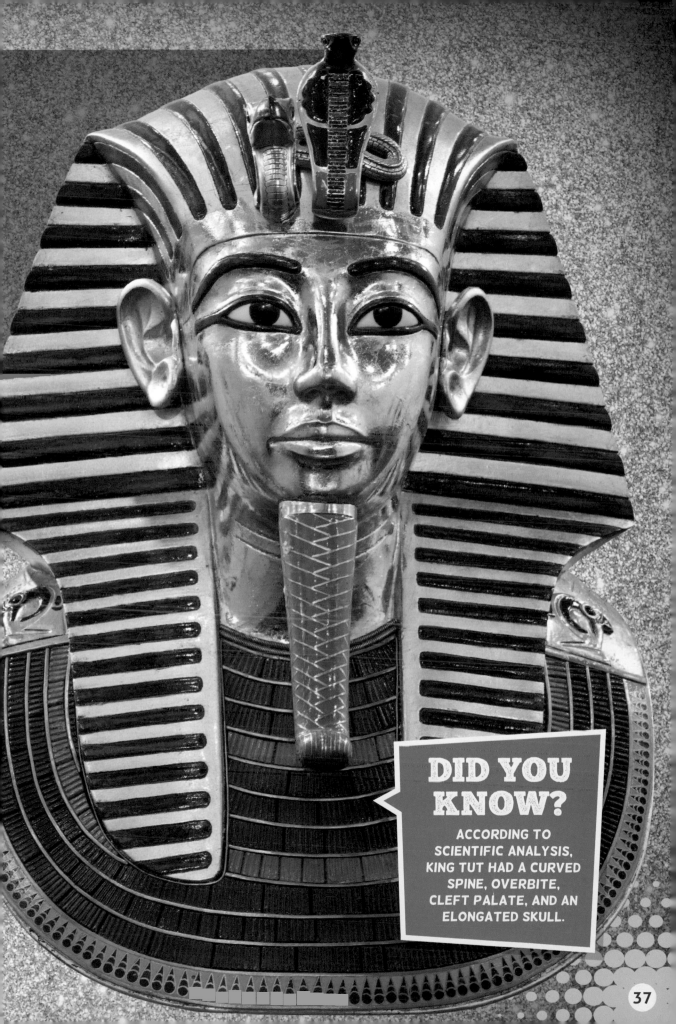

DID YOU KNOW?

ACCORDING TO SCIENTIFIC ANALYSIS, KING TUT HAD A CURVED SPINE, OVERBITE, CLEFT PALATE, AND AN ELONGATED SKULL.

New Kingdom: Ramses II

In 1279 BCE, more than 40 years after King Tut's death, Ramses II became pharaoh. He ruled 66 years—the longest of any Egyptian pharaoh. Like Hatshepsut, Ramses II expanded Egypt's territory through war. His empire stretched to the Mediterranean Sea where it bordered a longtime enemy, the Hittites. Ramses II built many temples during his reign and even restored the Great Sphinx, which was built over one thousand years before his reign. Ramses II reigned until 1213 BCE when he was more than 90 years old.

ABU SIMBEL

Abu Simbel was built by Ramses II in a remote location, deep in Nubia. Its location is well beyond the boundaries that make up ancient Egypt. Abu Simbel was constructed in the cliffs by the Nile. Construction began in 1264 BCE and lasted 20 years. The site is made up of two temples, the larger of which was dedicated to several gods, and the smaller was built for Ramses II's wife, Nefertari.

The main hall of the larger temple was decorated with painted battle scenes against the Hittites. The temple was specially constructed so that twice a year the Sun would illuminate statues inside the inner sanctuary. The inner sanctuary had statues of Ramses II among statues of three gods. The placement allowed three of the statues, including Ramses II, to be lit up by the Sun, while the god of the underworld was left in shadow. The exterior of the temple also featured four colossal statues of Ramses II that were each 66 feet tall. Each statues' ears measured three feet long!

DID YOU KNOW?

IN THE 1960S, ABU SIMBEL WAS UNDER THREAT OF FLOOD FROM THE BUILDING OF THE ASWAN DAM WHICH CREATED LAKE NASSER, AN ARTIFICIAL RESERVOIR. WITH THE HELP OF 2,000 ENGINEERS AND CONTRACTORS, ABU SIMBEL WAS DISMANTLED AND RELOCATED TO AN ARTIFICIAL HILL SAFE FROM LAKE NASSER'S WATERS.

New Kingdom: Cleopatra

Alexander the Great

After Ramses II's death, ancient Egypt was never the same, and around 1070 BCE a series of foreign rulers took over Egypt. One of the most famous foreign rulers, Alexander the Great, the king of Macedonia, conquered Egypt. After Alexander the Great's death, the Macedonians continued to rule Egypt. Cleopatra was the last of the Macedonian rulers of Egypt.

Cleopatra was born in Egypt, but she was Macedonian, or Greek, and most likely had no Egyptian blood. She spoke Greek and followed Greek customs, but as pharaoh she learned the Egyptian language and adopted Egyptian customs. Because she was a member of a ruling family, Cleopatra went to school and studied history, science, medicine, and math.

Cleopatra became pharaoh at the age of eighteen with her ten-year-old brother, Ptolemy XIII, when their father, Ptolemy XII, died. She was shunned by Ptolemy XIII's advisors, who wanted him to rule, and she was forced to flee to Syria. In Syria, she built an army and attacked her brother's army back in Egypt with the help of Julius Caesar, a powerful Roman leader. Cleopatra's brother drowned and died in the battle. With Caesar's defeat of Cleopatra's brother, she became pharaoh and wanted to maintain Egypt's independence from the aggressive Roman Empire.

Julius Caesar

Cleopatra was an intelligent and cunning ruler who had relationships with Julius Caesar, and another Roman leader, Mark Antony. At different times during Cleopatra's life, both men protected her throne and ensured she remained pharaoh. When Caesar died, Cleopatra had a relationship with Mark Antony.

Mark Antony

When Mark Antony heard that Cleopatra had died he was so upset that he killed himself, even though the rumor about Cleopatra was false. Cleopatra was so devastated by Mark Antony's death that she closed herself in a chamber where it is believed she later died from a venomous snake bite. However, some scholars argue that she didn't die from a snake bite because a cobra would have been too big to smuggle inside a basket like the story suggests. Instead, scholars speculate that she may have been murdered. After Cleopatra's death, Egypt became part of the Roman Empire.

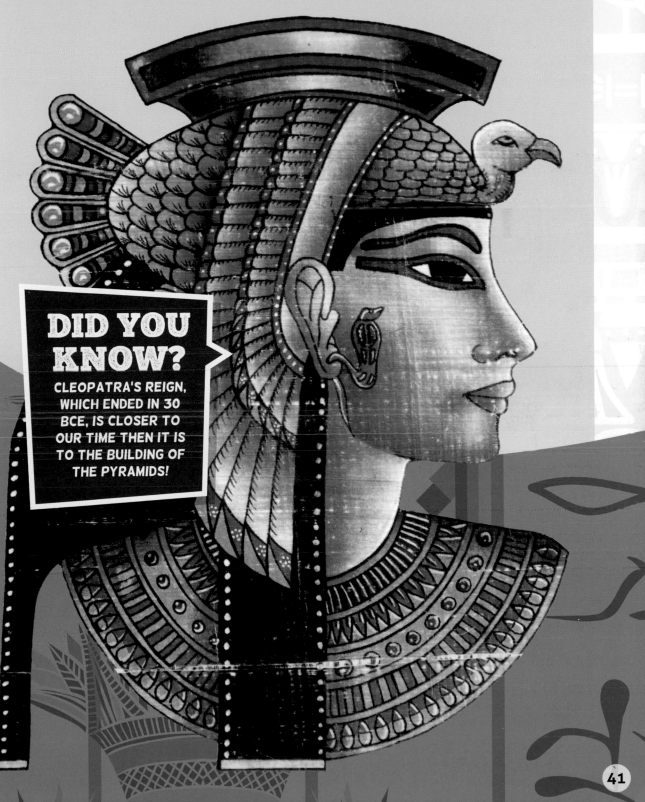

DID YOU KNOW?

CLEOPATRA'S REIGN, WHICH ENDED IN 30 BCE, IS CLOSER TO OUR TIME THEN IT IS TO THE BUILDING OF THE PYRAMIDS!

Uncovering Egypt: Napoleon

Even though Egypt's influence on the modern world can be traced back thousands of years, ancient Egypt was relatively unknown until the end of the eighteenth century. That changed drastically when Napoleon Bonaparte landed in Egypt.

Napoleon Bonaparte was a general and eventually emperor of France in the nineteenth century. In 1798, Napoleon and 37,000 troops invaded Egypt. Scholars believe that Napoleon's invasion of Egypt was a way to block Britain's trade route to India. The invasion also highlighted Napoleon's dominance and power.

In addition to troops, Napoleon's excursion included 150 scholars that consisted of archaeologists, scientists, engineers, architects, geographers, and more. Even though Napoleon's military campaign was a failure, his scholarly excursion was very successful.

Scholars collected plant and mineral samples, studied native animals, and sketched temples and monuments. Ancient Egypt was uncovered and the temples and tombs of Luxor, Philae, Dendera, and the Valley of the Kings were documented.

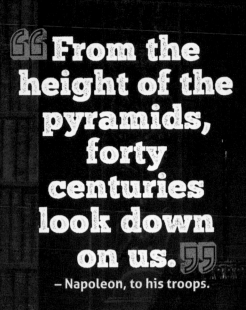

> ❝ **From the height of the pyramids, forty centuries look down on us.** ❞
>
> – Napoleon, to his troops.

Napoleon's scholars wanted to find a way to share their discoveries with a wider audience, so they decided to publish their findings. In 1809, *Description of Egypt* was published and by 1828, twenty-three volumes were added to the collection. The volumes of antiquities included sketches and descriptions of artifacts, temples, and monuments uncovered during Napoleon's excursion.

For the first time, an extensive encyclopedia covering ancient Egypt was created and accessible to many people. Europeans began viewing Egypt as exotic and as a place of mysteries. Soon interest in ancient Egypt spread all over Europe and the United States.

The Discovery of Abu Simbel

After Napoleon's Egyptian campaign, interest in Egypt was in full force. In 1813, Swiss explorer Johann Ludwig Burckhardt sailed down the Nile and landed on the river's bank in Nubia, southern Egypt. He was accompanied by his Egyptian guide, Saad, to explore the temple of Nefertari, which was believed to be the only temple at the site.

Once Burckhardt landed on the Nile's shore, he decided to walk south, where he noticed the tops of four colossal statue heads peeking out of the sand. He had rediscovered the temple of Abu Simbel, which had been buried in the sand for hundreds of years! The colossal heads in the sand belonged to statues of Ramses II. In addition to the large statues of himself, smaller statues of Ramses II's wife and children were also featured in the front of the temple.

Burckhardt told another explorer, Giovanni Battista Belzoni, about the temple he uncovered. After Burckhardt's death in 1817, Belzoni made the journey down the Nile and found Abu Simbel. Over 30 feet of sand covered the temple's entrance, so Belzoni began sweeping it away. However, the project was much bigger than expected so Belzoni was unable to clear away all the sand. In 1909, all of the sand covering the façade of Abu Simbel was completely removed.

Jean-François Champollion, Thomas Young, and the Rosetta Stone

Around twenty years after the discovery of the Rosetta Stone, French historian and **philologist** Jean-François Champollion finally cracked the mysterious hieroglyphs carved in the stone. At a young age, Champollion was fascinated by language. By sixteen years old, he had mastered six ancient languages. His next task was to uncover the mysterious language on the Rosetta Stone. However, Champollion wouldn't have been able to interpret the Rosetta Stone without Englishman Thomas Young's discovery in 1814.

While on vacation, Thomas Young brought a copy of the text on the Rosetta Stone with him. He focused on a set of hieroglyphs surrounded by a loop called a **cartouche**. Since he was familiar with the Greek version of the text, he assumed it must be an important name, such as Ptolemy. He was able to match symbols in the name with the phonetics in Ptolemy. Although he gave up on deciphering hieroglyphs further, the interpretation of "Ptolemy" paved the way for Champollion to fully understand the Rosetta Stone.

Stone Translation

The Rosetta Stone was the perfect object for Champollion to translate since it included the same text in three languages. While studying the three languages on the Rosetta Stone, Champollion noticed similarities between the hieroglyphic and non-hieroglyphic texts. He noted that some of the hieroglyphs were alphabetic, some were phonetic, and some represented whole words. Champollion published papers that listed his findings, the hieroglyphs he translated, and their Greek equivalents.

DID YOU KNOW?

IN 1827, LEGEND SAYS THAT CHAMPOLLION SHOUTED "I'VE GOT IT!" TO HIS BROTHER WHEN HE FINALLY DECODED THE ROSETTA STONE. HIS EXCITEMENT CAUSED HIM TO FAINT AND HE WAS BEDRIDDEN FOR SEVERAL DAYS AFTER HIS FINDINGS.

Champollion's deciphering of the Rosetta Stone was a monumental moment in Egyptology. In fact, he is often called the "Father of Egyptology," since he provided the foundation for scholars to truly understand ancient Egypt.

Howard Carter and King Tut

One of the most important findings in Egyptology occurred in 1922 in the Valley of Kings when Howard Carter swept aside dirt revealing a series of steps. Howard Carter was an English Egyptologist who got his start in Egypt in 1891 at just seventeen years old. His father, an English artist, had his son accompany an archaeologist and sketch his findings. In 1907, Carter was introduced to the wealthy Lord Carnarvon who was an amateur Egyptologist. Lord Carnarvon sought an Egyptian expedition that he could support financially, and Howard Carter was the perfect person for him to send to Egypt.

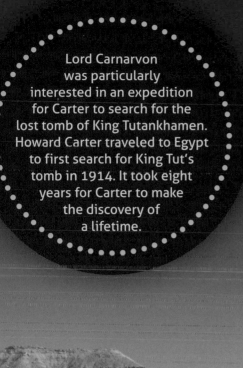

Lord Carnarvon was particularly interested in an expedition for Carter to search for the lost tomb of King Tutankhamen. Howard Carter traveled to Egypt to first search for King Tut's tomb in 1914. It took eight years for Carter to make the discovery of a lifetime.

In November 1922, Carter discovered steps in the Valley of the Kings that served as the entrance to a tomb. He frantically sent a telegram to England to let Lord Carnarvon know of the discovery. Lord Carnarvon traveled to Egypt—which took 15 days—and joined Carter so they could open the entrance together.

The initial passageway was covered in stone and rubble. Carter and Lord Carnarvon cleared it and continued to a sealed door at the end of the hallway. Carter cut a hole in the plaster and stuck a burning candle up to the hole. Lord Carnarvon asked if he saw anything through the hole, to which Carter replied, "Yes, wonderful things."

King Tut's Tomb

King Tut's tomb, his resting place for 3,000 years, was composed of a four-room chamber. The rooms were full of golden chariots, precious jewels, gold, miniature ships, toys, perfume, jewelry, and much more. It took Carter ten years to catalog the thousands of objects buried with King Tut. Of course, one of the most magnificent discoveries was the sarcophagus that held the pharaoh's body.

The sarcophagus included three layered coffins. The outer two coffins were made of wood and covered in gold and jewels. Beneath these two coffins was a solid gold coffin that held King Tut's body. Like almost all pharaohs, King Tut was mummified after his death. A death mask was placed over his face and showed King Tut in the image of a god. It also included the crook and flail which were symbols of a pharaoh's right to rule. The back of the death mask was engraved with a spell from *The Book of the Dead* that would ensure King Tut's safe journey to the afterlife.

Many scholars view the discovery of King Tut's tomb as important not necessarily because of King Tut's reign, but rather because of the treasure trove discovered there. Each object was a piece of history that illustrated ancient Egyptians' values and their complex beliefs about death.

MUMMY'S CURSE?

Shortly after the opening of King's Tut's tomb, Lord Carnarvon was bitten by a mosquito. While shaving, he nicked the bite, which resulted in a serious infection. Just three weeks after laying his eyes on the tomb's treasure and splendor, Lord Carnarvon died. Many newspapers called his death the "Mummy's Curse"! They believed he died because he disturbed the king's tomb and final resting place.

The Unfinished Obelisk

In Aswan, along the Nile River in southern Egypt, a colossal obelisk rests in the sand. Obelisks are giant four-sided stone columns with pyramidal tops. They were commissioned by pharaohs as monuments that celebrated the pharaoh's rule and achievements. They were often inscribed with hieroglyphs.

The obelisk was believed to be commissioned by Hatshepsut or Thutmose III. Aswan was chosen as the location for the carving of the obelisk, since it was home to large granite quarries. The obelisk was carved out of the bedrock and was planned to be hoisted up and brought to the Nile where it could be transported to its final location, the temple of Amon at Thebes. However, at a late stage in the carving, the project was abandoned because the granite cracked. If the obelisk had been finished, it would have stood 137 feet tall and weighed over one thousand tons.

In 1922, shortly after Howard Carter discovered King Tut's tomb, Egyptologist Rex Engelbach uncovered what is known today as the "unfinished obelisk." When Engelbach stumbled upon the obelisk it was covered in debris—he was very surprised and ecstatic to find he'd discovered the remains of a large project abandoned 2,500 years previous.

When Engelbach fully uncovered and removed the sand covering the obelisk, he wanted to figure out how long it would have taken workers to carve it. So, he decided to put it to the test by carving into a fresh slab of granite himself. After hours of chipping into the granite, Engelbach calculated that it would have taken each worker approximately 12 hours to carve one inch into the granite. It would have taken a year and a half for the carving to be complete, which would have then been followed up with months of polishing.

Ship for a Pharaoh

In 1954, Egyptian archaeologist Kamel El Mallakh was excavating near the Great Pyramids. He decided to dig under a stone wall near Khufu's pyramid. While he was digging in the dirt, he noticed wood chips and charcoal. He dug further and hit limestone blocks—40 of them—that were used to cover a deep pit. Mallakh decided to dig through one of the limestone blocks where he uncovered one of the most amazing discoveries of the twentieth century: pharaoh Khufu's ship.

Below the limestone blocks, Mallakh saw wooden planks, ropes, oars, and smelled the strong scent of cedar. He was viewing the parts and pieces of Khufu's 144-feet long ship that had been buried since approximately 2500 BCE. It took Mallakh more than two years to uncover the 1,224 pieces that made up the ship. Haj Youssef, a chief restorer at the Egyptian Department of Antiquities, assembled and rebuilt the ship.

The
boat was
disassembled and
buried next to Khufu's
pyramid so it could be used
in the afterlife. The workers
made reassembly easy for the
afterlife by labeling the ship's
pieces and essentially
creating instructions
for assembly.

The
superbly-built
ship was constructed
from cedar—a type of wood
that was not found in Egypt—it
would have been transported all
the way from Lebanon, hundreds of
miles away. The ship included a
30-foot long deckhouse and 12 oars.
No nails were used to construct the
ship, but rather rope was used
in a way that the boat was
"sewn" together.

The ship was most likely symbolic of the god Ra's sun boat, and was meant as a vessel to carry Khufu to the afterlife. The discovery of Khufu's ship exemplified ancient Egyptian engineering and technology. Even though it wasn't meant to sail down the Nile, its construction was so precise that it could have easily sailed on water. In 1984, the assembled ship was placed inside the Khufu Boat Museum which stands near the Great Pyramid of Giza.

Khufu Boat Museum

Tools of the Trade

When they aren't teaching, writing, researching, or curating, Egyptologists are in the field digging. First, they must decide on an area that they think is a promising site for artifacts. Equipment and staff are brought to the excavation site and a small camp is set up with everything the crew will need for excavation. Then it's time to dig in! The crew starts small by scooping up and sifting small amounts of dirt to look for artifacts. If any objects are found, they are photographed and recorded. The process can be slow and even just a small area can take weeks and months to search through.

Trowel

Trowels are small hand tools used for digging, scraping, and smoothing. It is the same tool that masons use when laying bricks. Trowels help Egyptologists gently scrape away dirt. The pointed ends of some trowels help dig deeper in the sand and dirt.

Brushes

Brushes are useful tools at an excavation site because they sweep away any loose dirt without damaging fragile artifacts.

Dustpans and Wheelbarrows

Dustpans are used to sweep up dirt that has already been searched through. This dirt is then transported to a wheelbarrow where larger amounts of dirt are discarded. This ensures that Egyptologists aren't looking through the same dirt more than once.

Screens

Instead of picking through dirt for larger pieces, Egyptologists use a screen to put larger amounts of dirt on. The holes in the screen allow small grains of sand to fall through the screen while capturing any larger objects.

DID YOU KNOW?

MANY OF THE EXCAVATION TOOLS USED BY EGYPTOLOGISTS ARE BASIC TOOLS LIKE THE ONES FOUND IN A HOUSEHOLD GARAGE. OTHERS ARE MORE ADVANCED.

Satellites

Although Egyptologists today still use many of the same types of tools that nineteenth-century Egyptologists used, technology has helped make digs a bit easier. Imaging satellites are objects that orbit Earth taking pictures. Egyptologists can use these images to gain a better understanding of an area. In 2017, Egyptologist Sarah Parcak discovered 3,000 ancient Egyptian settlements by using satellite imagery.

Amazing Ancient Egypt

For hundreds of years, remnants of a civilization that lasted 3,000 years lay buried under the desert sand. Although tombs and monuments were plundered and raided throughout history, it wasn't until Egyptologists made major discoveries, such as the discovery and translation of the Rosetta Stone, that the secrets of the ancient civilization were unlocked. Finally, the **cryptic** symbols that covered tomb walls, monuments, and papyrus were translated and the intricacies of ancient Egyptians' beliefs and customs came to life.

From Johann Ludwig Burckhardt to Howard Carter, Egyptologists' findings have shaped our understanding of ancient Egypt and how the advanced civilization has influenced our lives today. From the Washington Monument in Washington, D.C., to modern calendars to mathematics, aspects of ancient Egypt are present in our everyday lives.

Today, excavations are constantly taking place in Egypt and everyday there's a possibility for the next great discovery. Perhaps you're the next great Egyptologist— all you have to do is dig in.

Quiz

1 What important river made life in ancient Egypt possible?

    a) Amazon River
    b) Nile River
    c) Volga River
    d) Congo River

2 Which discovery helped scholars interpret hieroglyphs?

    a) Rosetta Stone
    b) King Tut's tomb
    c) *The Book of the Dead*
    d) Luxor Temple

3 What was the purpose of *The Book of the Dead*?

    a) It taught people how to build tombs
    b) It listed graves in a cemetery
    c) It helped the deceased safely get to the afterlife
    d) It outlined how to communicate with the dead

4 During mummification, which organ was left inside the body?

    a) Brain
    b) Intestines
    c) Heart
    d) Liver

5 Why were pyramids built?

a) For tombs for the pharaohs
b) As markets for goods to be sold
c) For schools where scribes learned to write
d) To worship Cleopatra

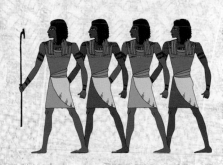

6 After Cleopatra's death, what empire did Egypt become part of?

a) British Empire
b) French Empire
c) Greek Empire
d) Roman Empire

7 Which Egyptologist discovered King Tut's tomb?

a) Napoleon
b) Howard Carter
c) Kamel El Mallakh
d) Jean-François Champollion

8 What do Egyptologists NOT use when digging?

a) Trowels
b) Satellites
c) Screens
d) Axes

Glossary

artifact: an object made by a human

cryptic: having a mysterious and unclear meaning

cartouche: an oval or rectangular shape surrounding hieroglyphs

dynasty: a line of rulers related to one another

Egyptology: study of ancient Egyptian artifacts and way of life

civilization: the way of life, including technology, arts, and government, of a group of people

embalmer: person that prepares a dead body so it doesn't decay

equator: an imaginary line that runs around the world and splits it into northern and southern hemispheres